I am a

R
CA

I am a ROMAN CATHOLIC

Brenda Pettenuzzo
meets
Miriam Braham

Photography: Chris Fairclough

Religious Consultant: Father George Stokes

W
FRANKLIN WATTS
LONDON • SYDNEY

Miriam Braham is nine years old.
She and her family live on the border
of London with Essex. Her father,
Warren, is a partner in a small
business. Her mother, Sue, is a
drama teacher. Miriam has one
brother, Adam, who is eight years
old. They both attend St Joseph's
Roman Catholic Primary School.

Contents

© 1985 Franklin Watts
This edition 2001

Franklin Watts
96 Leonard Street
London EC2A 4XD

Franklin Watts Australia
56 O'Riordan Street
Alexandria, Sydney, NSW 2015

ISBN 0 7496 4178 9

Text Editor: Chester Fisher
Design: Edward Kinsey
Illustration: Tony Payne

Photograph: Arturo Mari 7.

Printed in Hong Kong

The publishers would like to thank
the Braham family and the
congregation of St Mary's and
St Ethelburga's.

10 9 8 7 6 5 4 3 2 1

What Catholics believe

Roman Catholics are Christians. That means we are followers of Jesus Christ.

The Christian Church has three main parts – Roman Catholic, Protestant and Orthodox. All Christians believe in one God. They believe that God sent His son to live as a man. He was called Jesus. He spent three years teaching and doing wonderful things. He was put to death on a cross but Christians believe that He came back from the dead.

The Pope is the leader of all Roman Catholics. Jesus made his disciple, Peter, the first Pope.

Peter became the first Pope when Jesus said: "You are Peter, and on this rock I will build my Church." Peter means 'rock'. Pope John Paul II is his modern successor. He is helped by Bishops, who each look after an area called a Diocese. This is split into smaller areas called Parishes, looked after by a Parish Priest.

Going to Church

Our Church is called St Mary's and St Ethelburga's. As we go in we make the sign of the cross with Holy Water.

The Parish Church is the heart of the Catholic Community. There is Holy Water near the entrance. As people go in they dip the fingers of their right hands into the water and mark a cross upon themselves with it. The Cross is the sign of Christianity. Doing this reminds them of their Baptism, when they joined the Church.

Most of the activities in our Church take place around the Altar. Next to it is the Tabernacle.

The Altar is really a big table. The people gather around it for the Mass. The Tabernacle (right) holds the Blessed Sacrament – the Risen Jesus in the form of bread. Catholics believe that God is everywhere but this special place is kept in every church. A light burns there to remind people of God's presence.

Sunday Mass

We go to Mass on Sundays. The Priest wears special clothes called vestments.

The Mass is a celebration of the last meal which Jesus shared with His friends – the Last Supper. The Priest's vestments or robes vary according to the time of year or festival. The Mass has several parts. First the congregation asks forgiveness for its sins. There is often a prayer of praise, readings from the Bible and a talk by the Priest.

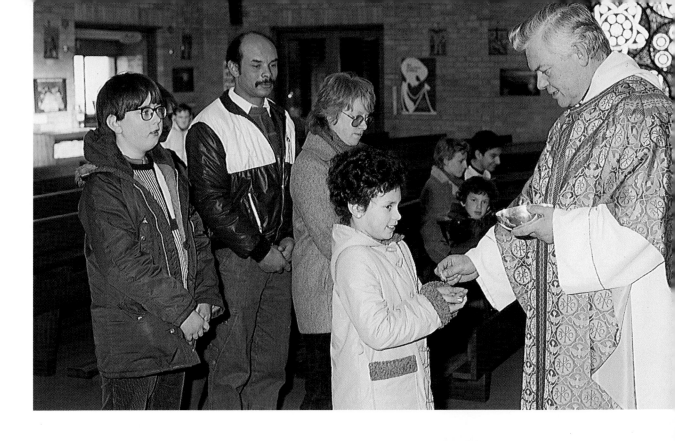

The Priest does what Jesus did at the Last Supper. We take part in it by receiving Holy Communion.

The Priest takes bread and wine and uses the same words that Jesus used at the Last Supper. Catholics believe that the special bread, called the Host, and the wine actually become the Risen Jesus. Catholics can receive Jesus in this special way as Holy Communion. The Mass ends with a blessing from the Priest. After Mass people stop to chat with the Priest and their friends.

First Communion

When I made by first Communion, I wore a special dress. My family and friends came to a party afterwards.

When Miriam was seven, she was allowed to take Communion for the first time. In school, her class prepared for this in their religious education lessons. At home she prepared with her parents. One Sunday there was a special celebration Mass. This was a very important step in Miriam's life as a Catholic.

Miriam Braham
received
the Blessed Eucharist
for the first time

in SS. Mary and Ethelburga's

on Sunday 15th May 1983

Father John Dudley

Confession

I go to Confession if I feel that I have done something wrong.

Catholics believe that God is like a kind father, always ready to forgive. They talk to a Priest when they are sorry for doing wrong. The Priest sits in a very small room called a Confessional. Catholics then "make up" with God. This is called Reconciliation.

Mary, the Mother of Jesus

We use Rosary beads when we say the Hail Mary, a special prayer for Mary.

Roman Catholics have a special devotion to Mary. This is because she was the mother of Jesus, and because she did exactly what God asked of her. Most churches have pictures or statues of her like the ones seen opposite. The Rosary is a special devotion to Mary in which prayers are said while thinking about the important things which happened to her and to Jesus.

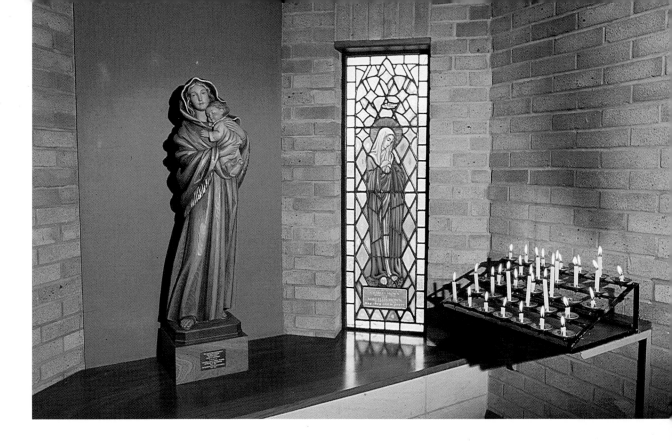

The Saints

Saint Ethelburga is our patron saint. She lived a long time ago and was a very holy person.

There are many Saints recognized by the Roman Catholic Church. They are all people who have lived very special lives. The Church spends a long time making sure that each one is special enough before declaring them a Saint. Many people are devoted to particular Saints, and ask them for help in becoming closer to God.

ST. ETHELBURGA

The history of Miriam's family

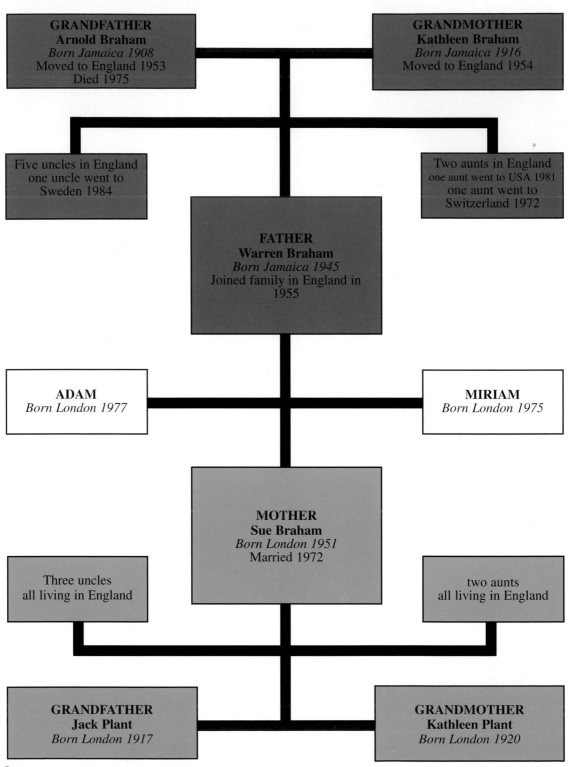

GRANDFATHER
Arnold Braham
Born Jamaica 1908
Moved to England 1953
Died 1975

GRANDMOTHER
Kathleen Braham
Born Jamaica 1916
Moved to England 1954

Five uncles in England
one uncle went to
Sweden 1984

Two aunts in England
one aunt went to USA 1981
one aunt went to
Switzerland 1972

FATHER
Warren Braham
Born Jamaica 1945
Joined family in England in
1955

ADAM
Born London 1977

MIRIAM
Born London 1975

MOTHER
Sue Braham
Born London 1951
Married 1972

Three uncles
all living in England

two aunts
all living in England

GRANDFATHER
Jack Plant
Born London 1917

GRANDMOTHER
Kathleen Plant
Born London 1920

16

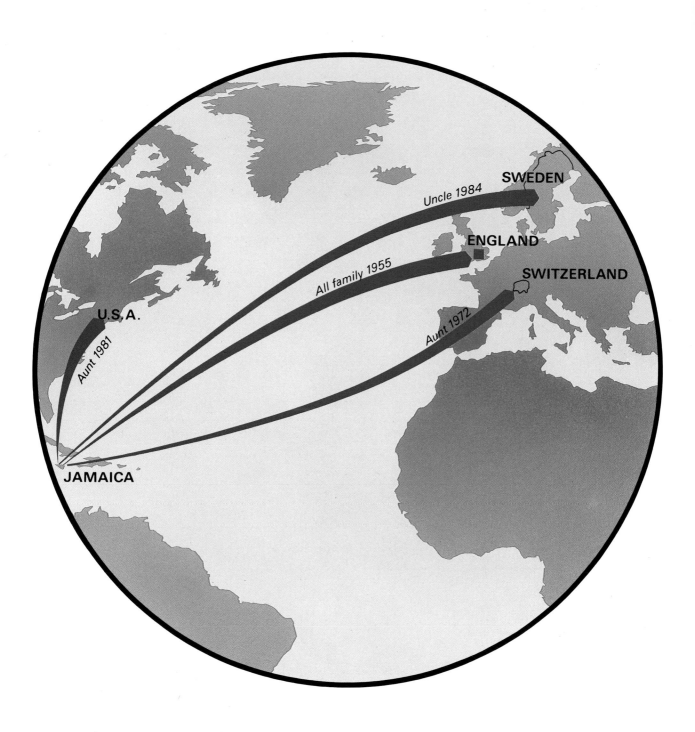

Going to a Catholic school

My school is named after Saint Joseph. We learn all the normal subjects but we also learn about our Roman Catholic faith.

At school, Miriam learns about being a Christian and a Roman Catholic. Her class has religious education lessons with their class teacher. Sometimes the Parish Priest celebrates Mass in the classroom for the children and their parents.

**My parents help me to
learn about my faith as well. We
have lots of books at home.**

Some people decide to become
Catholics when they are grown up.
Most Catholics are like Miriam and
Adam – they joined the Church as
babies and learned about it from
their parents. Not all Catholic
children are able to go to Catholic
schools so it is important to learn at
home.

Advent and Christmas

During Advent we prepare for the birthday of Jesus – Christmas. We have an Advent wreath at Church.

The season of Advent is the beginning of the Church year. The Advent Wreath, with one candle for each of the four Sundays of Advent, reminds everyone that Christmas is approaching. Each Sunday, one more candle is lighted and on Christmas day the central one is lit. This is a reminder that Christ is the Light of the World.

Christmas is a happy time for us and we decorate our house to celebrate. We always have a creche like the one in the stable where Jesus was born.

All Christians believe that Jesus was born in a stable even though he was the Son of God. The story of Jesus was not written down until many years later, so very little is known about his childhood. His first visitors were shepherds, and wise men from far away. These can all be seen worshipping at the creche.

Lent and Easter

Ash Wednesday is the start of Lent. The Priest marks our foreheads with Ashes.

During the six weeks of Lent, Catholics prepare for Easter. The marking of foreheads with ashes is a sign of turning to God and away from everyday things which do not last. During Lent, Catholics try to pray more, and to do things that will help other people.

On Palm Sunday we are all given palms at Church. I put them on my wall at home.

Palm Sunday is the beginning of Holy Week – the most important part of the Christian Year. Palms were waved when Jesus rode into Jerusalem. The next week He died and rose from the dead. Ceremonies on Thursday and Friday commemorate what happened at that time. On Saturday night at the Easter Vigil Mass, everyone repeats their Baptism promises. A new Easter Candle burns to show that Jesus Christ drives out the darkness.

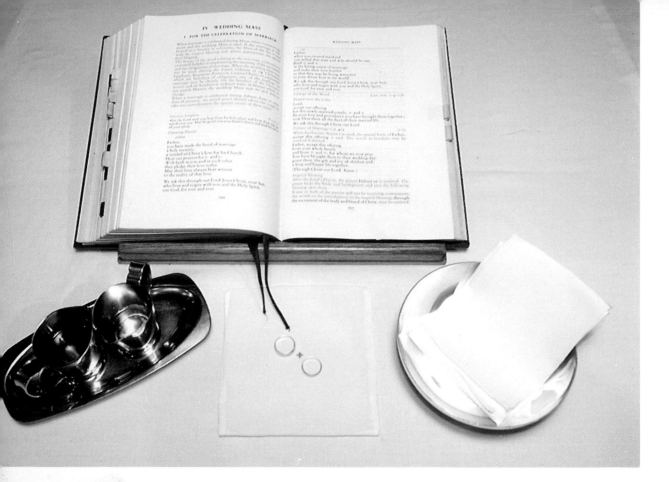

Weddings

At a wedding the bride and groom give rings to each other.

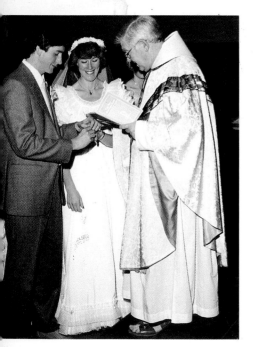

Roman Catholics usually ask for God's blessing on their marriage by having their wedding in church. Their friends and relations take part in the ceremony. Sometimes it forms part of a Mass. A priest officiates at the wedding. Roman Catholic Priests do not get married. They receive a Sacrament called Holy Orders.

Baptism

When I was a baby, my parents and godparents took me to church for my baptism. That was how I joined the Christian family.

At Baptism, babies have Holy Water poured on their heads. They are anointed with oil, and their parents hold a lighted candle and a white cloth for them. These are all signs of starting a new life with God. Baptism is a Sacrament, an outward sign of God's Grace to His people.

Miriam Kathleen Braham was Baptised on 7th September 1975 at Ss Mary and Ethelburga

Godparents: Catherine Jones Russell Braham

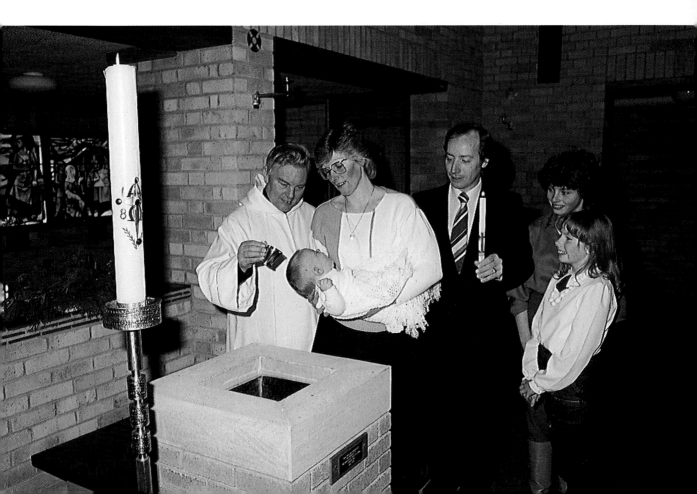

Preparing for Confirmation

Each of these candles belongs to one of the young people who are going to be confirmed. We are all praying for them.

Miriam did not choose to be baptized. Her parents chose for her. When she is older, she will be invited to join the Catholic Church as an adult. If she decides to do this she will receive the Sacrament of Confirmation from the Bishop. This "confirms" the promises which were made for her when she was baptized. Miriam sometimes buys books from the Church shop to learn more about her belief.

When we pray we are talking to God. We believe that He is like a loving father, and always has time to listen.

Miriam and Adam learn more and more about God and about being Catholics as they get older. They read books suggested by their parents and the priest. Sometimes they pray to God by saying well known prayers, and sometimes they pray in their own words.

The Roman Catholic Year

The Church year is based on the normal calendar year but starts with the Season of Advent at the end of November/ beginning of December. Apart from the major festivals there are many feast days devoted to the Saints who died on these days or dedicated to special events.

DECEMBER

NOVEMBER

OCTOBER

SEPTEMBER

AUGUST

JULY

CHRISTMAS DAY
25th December
Celebrates the birth of Jesus Christ.

ADVENT
November/December
The four Sundays before Christmas. A time of preparation and waiting for the birth of Jesus Christ.

ALL SAINTS DAY
1st November
Feast day

ASSUMPTION
15th August
A feast day which remembers Mary's reception into Heaven.

JANUARY

FEBRUARY

MARCH

APRIL

MAY

JUNE

EPIPHANY
6th January
Remembers the Visit of the three Magi (kings or wise men) to the newly-born Jesus Christ.

LENT
46 days
Begins on Ash Wednesday and ends at Easter. A time of prayer, fasting and preparation for the events of Easter.

ANNUNCIATION
25th March
The feast day which remembers the day on which Mary learned of her future role as the Mother of Jesus.

HOLY WEEK
begins with Passion or Palm Sunday which commemorates Jesus' entry into Jerusalem. Holy Thursday remembers the Last Supper of Jesus with His friends. Good Friday was the day on which Christ was crucified.

EASTER
50 days
This season begins on Easter Sunday and ends at Pentecost (Whitsun). Easter Sunday was when Jesus Christ rose from the dead. Ascension Thursday, when he returned to Heaven, is forty days later. At Pentecost, 10 days later, the Holy Spirit gave strength to Jesus' followers.

ST PETER and ST PAUL
29th June
Feast Day commemorating St Peter, the first Pope, and St Paul, writer of most of the letters in the New Testament to early Christians.

The dates of Lent and Easter change each year according to the date of Good Friday which is the Friday following the first full moon after the Spring Equinox. Good Friday is usually in April.

29

Facts and Figures

The Christian Church has about 1,000 million members in almost every part of the world. Of these about 700 million are Roman Catholics. In Britain there are about 7 million members of Christian churches. About 2 million are Roman Catholics.

Roman Catholicism began with the first followers of Jesus Christ. Jesus was a Jew who lived in the country which we now call Israel, about 2,000 years ago. He lived a very quiet life until He was about 30. Then He began to travel around the country teaching and performing miracles. He upset the Jewish leaders of the time, and they had Him crucified. This was a very painful death. Roman Catholics and other Christians believe that two days after the Crucifixion Jesus had conquered death by rising from His tomb.

At a later time, when Jesus' earthly body had returned to Heaven, His followers were given strength by the Holy Spirit to go out into the world and tell people about Jesus. This event was called Pentecost.

Most of the knowledge about Jesus comes from a part of the Bible called the New Testament. Stories about Jesus were passed on from person to person and finally written down some years later as books called the Gospels. As the Christian faith spread, many letters were written by the first followers to new groups of Christians. These letters, called Epistles, are also in the New Testament.

Pope John Paul II is the 263rd successor to Saint Peter. He lives in the Vatican City which is in Rome, Italy. A very large church in the Vatican, St Peter's Basilica, is built on the site of St Peter's tomb. Catholics believe that St Peter continues to guide the Church through the Popes who have succeeded him.

Each time a Pope dies, the new Pope is chosen by the Cardinals, who all come to Rome for this purpose.

As well as their belief in Jesus Christ and the authority of the Pope, Roman Catholics are obliged to do certain things. They attend Mass on Sundays and certain other days in the year. Adults also fast, that is, eat very little, and abstain from meat or something which they enjoy doing on Ash Wednesday and Good Friday. Every Friday they try to do without something and instead do something positive for someone in need.

Glossary

Baptism The ceremony when a child is given its Christian name and received into the Church.

Bible The sacred writing of Christianity said to be the word of God. They are divided into two parts. The Old Testament dates back to early Jewish times, before the time of Christ. The New Testament contains the life and words of Jesus Christ.

Bishop A leading priest. Catholics believe that the power of Christ's original followers has been handed down to the Bishops. Each one looks after a Diocese and is responsible for all the Church affairs in that area.

Confirmation The ceremony when a Christian decides to "confirm" the promises made on his or her behalf at baptism.

Confession Talking to a priest about things which are thought to be wrong and asking for God's forgiveness.

Crucifixion The way in which Jesus Christ was put to death. He was nailed to a wooden cross and left to die.

Gospel One of the books of the New Testament. The word comes from an old word meaning "Good News" because the Gospels contain the Good News of Jesus Christ. There are four Gospels.

Holy Water Water, usually used for Baptism, which has been blessed by a Priest.

Mass The ceremony which remembers the last meal of Christ. The bread and wine of Holy Communion are the Body and Blood of the Risen Christ.

Priest A man who has taken Holy Orders. He is licensed by a Bishop to administer the Sacraments and say Mass. When a priest is made a priest, he is said to be Ordained. This is carried out by a Bishop.

Resurrection The event which took place on the third day after Jesus was crucified. Catholics and other Christians believe that Jesus was raised to new life by God the Father. This was a victory over sin and death.

Sacrament There are seven Sacraments: Baptism, Confirmation, Holy Communion (or Eucharist), Reconciliation, Marriage, Holy Orders and the Sacrament of the Sick. They are all outward signs of God's Grace towards the people who receive them.

Index